Just Like Mine

Richard Northcott

T0346929

Name _____

Age _____

Class _____

OXFORD

UNIVERSITY PRESS

OXFORD
UNIVERSITY PRESS

Great Clarendon Street, Oxford OX2 6DP

Oxford University Press is a department of the University of Oxford.
It furthers the University's objective of excellence in research, scholarship,
and education by publishing worldwide in

Oxford New York

Auckland Cape Town Dar es Salaam Hong Kong Karachi
Kuala Lumpur Madrid Melbourne Mexico City Nairobi
New Delhi Shanghai Taipei Toronto

With offices in

Argentina Austria Brazil Chile Czech Republic France Greece
Guatemala Hungary Italy Japan South Korea Poland Portugal
Singapore Switzerland Thailand Turkey Ukraine Vietnam

OXFORD and OXFORD ENGLISH are registered trade marks of
Oxford University Press in the UK and in certain other countries

ISBN: 978 0 19 440103 6

Printed in China

Illustrations by: Jan McCafferty
With thanks to Sally Spray for her contribution to this series

Reading Dolphins
Notes for teachers & parents

📖 Using the book

1 Begin by looking at the first story page (page 2). Look at the picture and ask questions about it. Then read the story text under the picture with your students. Use section 1 of the CD for this if possible.

2 Teach and check the understanding of any new vocabulary. Note that some of the words are in the **Picture Dictionary** at the back of the book.

3 Now look at the activities on the right-hand page. Show the example to the students and instruct them to complete the activities. This may be done individually, in pairs, or as a class.

4 Do the same for the remaining pages of the book.

5 Retell the whole story more quickly, reinforcing the new vocabulary. Section 2 of the CD can help with this.

6 If possible, listen to the expanded story (section 3 of the CD). The students should follow in their books.

7 When the book is finished, use the **Picture Dictionary** to check that students understand and remember new vocabulary. Section 4 of the CD can help with this.

💿 Using the CD

The CD contains four sections.

1 The story told slowly, with pauses. Use this during the first reading. It may also be used for "Listen and repeat" activities at any point.

2 The story told at normal speed. This should be used once the students have read the book for the first time.

3 The expanded story. The story is told in a longer version. This will help the students understand English when it is spoken faster, as they will now know the story and the vocabulary.

4 Vocabulary. Each word in the **Picture Dictionary** is spoken and then used in a simple sentence.

Bianca is a student in Grade Four.
She likes to wear beautiful clothes.
"Are these your sunglasses, Bianca?"
asks her teacher.
"Oh yes! My sunglasses."

Connect.

Her name
is Bianca. •

This is her
teacher. •

Bianca is
a student. •

Bianca is in
Grade Four. •

This is her
classroom. •

These are her
sunglasses. •

This is her
sweater. •

These are her
sneakers. •

"Mommy! Why are you wearing those sunglasses? They are just like mine!"

"I'm sorry, Bianca. Let's go shopping to make you happy."

Write.

jeans   sunglasses   sneakers
cap   sweater   backpack   hair

sunglasses

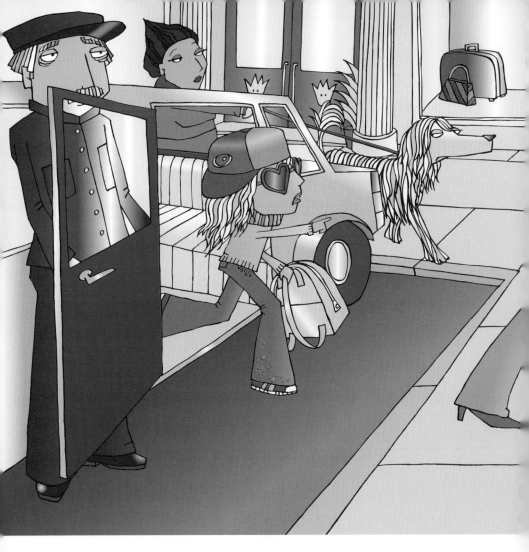

"Oh no! Look at that dog.
Its hair looks just like mine."
"I'm sorry, Miss," says the driver.
"I want to be special," says Bianca.

Write Yes, No or I don't know.

1 Bianca is at the supermarket.

No.

2 Bianca is getting out of the car.

_____

3 They are at the department store.

_____

4 Bianca has a brother.

_____

5 The driver is wearing a cap.

_____

6 Bianca has a dog.

_____

7 The car is blue.

_____

Bianca is looking at shoes.
"Mommy, look! Those sneakers are
just like mine!"
"I'm sorry, dear. Let's buy a new
pair for you."

Connect and answer the question.

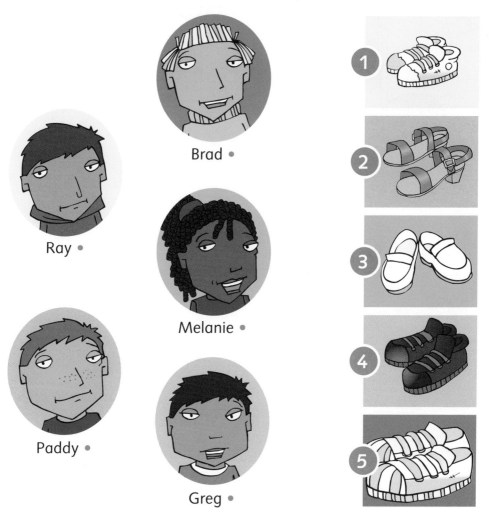

Brad •

Ray •

Melanie •

Paddy •

Greg •

1

2

3

4

5

Ray does not wear sandals.

Paddy, Brad, and Greg wear white shoes.

Brad and Greg's shoes are old.

Greg's shoes are the biggest.

Who has black sneakers? _____

"You see Mommy! That girl has a pink sweater. It's just like mine. I want a new sweater."

"All right, dear," says Mom.

How much are these? Write.

The sweater costs twenty-three dollars.
The socks cost two dollars.
The cap costs ten dollars.
The sneakers cost eighteen dollars.
The jeans cost twenty-one dollars
The backpack costs fifteen dollars.

"Why are you so unhappy, dear?"
"I want to be special Mommy, but
   I see many things just like mine."
"Don't be silly, Bianca."

Complete the sentences.

❶ We can buy
<u>T-shirts</u>
on the third floor.

❷ We can buy
_____
on the fourth floor.

❸ We can buy jeans on
the _____ .

❹ We can buy caps on
the _____ .

❺ We can buy _____ on
the first floor.

❻ We can buy sunglasses on the
_____ .

SILVERS
DEPARTMENT STORE

6th Floor   caps
5th Floor   sunglasses
4th Floor   sweaters
3rd Floor   T-shirts
2nd Floor   jeans
1st Floor   shoes

13

"See, Mommy. I am not silly.
Look at this doll. She has jeans just
like mine. I don't like this doll."
"I'm sorry, dear," says Mom.

Rearrange the words.

❶ is Bianca student a

Bianca is a student.

❷ to beautiful likes wear clothes she

❸ the store they in department are

❹ happy is not she

❺ wearing is Bianca jeans

❻ pair , the a jeans has of too doll

❼ jeans are Bianca's blue

"What do you want to buy,
Bianca?" asks Mom.
"I need a new cap because this man
has one just like mine."
"That's fine, dear," says Mom.

Answer the questions.

1. Where are Bianca and her mother?
   They're in the sports department.

2. What are they doing?

3. What is Bianca's mother buying?

4. How many rackets is she buying?

5. What does Bianca want to buy?

6. Why does she want to buy one?

7. What other sports equipment do you see?

8. What do you want to buy in this shop?

"Why aren't you drinking your juice, Bianca? It's very good."

"I don't want to drink it, Mommy. I am not thirsty."

"Are you sure, dear?"

Connect.

a Why aren't you drinking your juice?

1 It's broken.

b Why aren't you swimming?

2 It's too difficult.

c Why aren't you doing your homework?

3 I'm not thirsty.

d Why aren't you riding your bicycle?

4 It's too cold.

e Why aren't you eating?

5 I had a bad dream.

f Why aren't you sleeping?

6 I forgot it at home.

g Why aren't you reading your book?

7 I'm not hungry.

"It's time to go home, Bianca."

"Good idea, Mommy."

"Right. Let's go," says Mom.

"You see! That woman has a
  backpack just like mine."

What does Bianca see?
Put the sentences in order, 1 to 6.

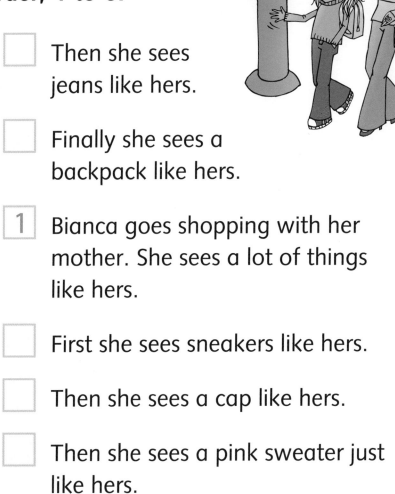

☐ Then she sees jeans like hers.

☐ Finally she sees a backpack like hers.

1 Bianca goes shopping with her mother. She sees a lot of things like hers.

☐ First she sees sneakers like hers.

☐ Then she sees a cap like hers.

☐ Then she sees a pink sweater just like hers.

"Excuse me. Is this your backpack?"
asks the woman.
"It looks just like mine," says Bianca.
"Yes, it is mine. Thank you."
"You're welcome."

Write the story.

This is a story about a ___girl___,

named _____. She is a _____

in Grade _____. She likes to wear

_____ clothes. She _____

want to be like other people. She likes to

be _____. Her _____ takes

her to the _____ store. Bianca is

very _____, because she sees

many people wearing things _____

like hers. Then, Bianca _____ a

woman with a _____ like hers.

She is _____ happy. The woman

_____ her the backpack. It is

_____ backpack. Bianca is a

_____ girl.

Picture Dictionary

backpack

dream

cap

driver

classroom

escalator

clothes

jeans

doll

money

racket

socks

sandals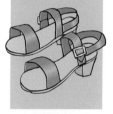

sunglasses

shoes

sweater

sneakers

T-shirt

Dolphin Readers

Dolphin Readers are available at five levels, from Starter to 4.

The Dolphins series covers four major themes:

Grammar, Living Together, The World Around Us, Science and Nature.

For each theme, there are two titles at every level.

Activity Books are available for all Dolphins.

All Dolphins are available on audio CD.
(2 TITLES ON EACH CD ⚪ SEE TABLE BELOW)

Teacher's Notes are available at **www.oup.com/elt/dolphins**

	Grammar	Living Together	The World Around Us	Science and Nature
Starter	• Silly Squirrel • Monkeying Around	• My Family • A Day with Baby	• Doctor, Doctor • Moving House	• A Game of Shapes • Baby Animals
Level 1	• Meet Molly • Where Is It?	• Little Helpers • Jack the Hero	• On Safari • Lost Kitten	• Number Magic • How's the Weather?
Level 2	• Double Trouble • Super Sam	• Candy for Breakfast • Lost!	• A Visit to the City • Matt's Mistake	• Numbers, Numbers Everywhere • Circles and Squares
Level 3	• Students in Space • What Did You Do Yesterday?	• New Girl in School • Uncle Jerry's Great Idea	• Just Like Mine • Wonderful Wild Animals	• Things That Fly • Let's Go to the Rainforest
Level 4	• The Tough Task • Yesterday, Today, and Tomorrow	• We Won the Cup • Up and Down	• Where People Live • City Girl, Country Boy	• In the Ocean • Go, Gorillas, Go